LOVE WORKS

A C K N O W L E D G M E N T S

Thank you, Mayor Willie L. Brown, Jr., for this appointment to the position of Poet Laureate of San Francisco. I am proud to hold this title in a city that inspires poetry, where progressive movements have been created and legends like Lawrence Ferlinghetti, our first Poet Laureate, can be righteously celebrated. Thanks also to the Poet Laureate Committee, the San Francisco Public Library, and the ArtCouncil.

I am immensely grateful to my husband, Cecil Williams, who each day transforms me with his love, my daugher Tianne, my mother, my friends in the Asian American community, and my Glide Memorial Church family. You have encouraged and supported me in my journey to be whole, to create poetry not separately from my work at Glide Church. You honor me and you nurture others to break silences, tell their stories, and sing from the margins and edges of society for justice, bread, and dignity.

To artists and writers of our diverse communities, to editors and coaches who have cast light upon the difficult and shadowed roads, my special thanks to you for inspiring me to discover new depths and heights in this continuing journey.

Finally, I extend gratitude to the City Lights Publishing family and editor Nancy J. Peters for producing the Poet Laureate Series and once again affirming the power of the Word.

TABLE OF CONTENTS

INAUGURAL ADDRESS
THE POWER OF POETRY

POETRY HAS THE POWER TO CONNECT US, TO TRANSFORM US.
In a poem to my mother I say:

> There are miracles that happen, she said,
> when the silence is broken, and all is made visible.
> These stories connect me with history,
> these words release me from cages of shame
> these poems break free from barbed-wire prisons.
> > We recognize ourselves at last.
> > We are unafraid.
> > Our language is beautiful.

Language. Poetry has been for me the language of my definition
and my liberation, although it has not always been so. It had

been my experience in school that poetry was esoteric – art elevated above life – rarefied and inaccessible. I wanted to redefine poetry as a means to connect with others, and to make poetry a bridge, spanning communities, ethnicities, continents. For me, poetry should be accessible, connecting our human experiences, steeped in the struggles that define us. Poetry gives form to the power of imagination and speaks as the conscience of real life. Elizabeth Catlett, renowned sculptor, and poets Lawrence Ferlinghetti and Pablo Neruda perhaps state best what I feel about poetry: that art is created both "in solitary and in solidarity." Poetry, for me, is the act of speaking the truth of the inner self and being connected to or informed by the community. Poetry is timeless, reaching through generations, across continents to my great-ancestors buried in ashes of Hiroshima, and to my grandmother in an Amache Gate Internment Camp. Poetry weeps in circles of famine in Rwanda and in circles of Argentine mothers of the disappeared.

Poetry opens the heart,
rises from the place of love and passion,
makes romance delicious,
puts vigor in our marching feet,
shakes our shoulders, straightens our spines,
moves our hands to clap in time.

Poetry inspires our children with visions in color
and memory and history.

When I run in the neighborhoods of San Francisco, I am
always reminded of why I love this City: its diversity. In the
poetry of each unique community are the echoes of past and
emerging songs.

City Lights in North Beach, Ferlinghetti's temple of poetry
& famous beats. I still hear Ginsberg's "Guru Ommmmm" in
an antinuclear drone.

Chinatown: Rhythms from Kearny Street Writers Workshop,
the ghost of I Hotel, and manong Freddie's banjo strums,
longing for a home. But it is the powerful year of the
Dragon, Chinese voices warn.

Mrs. Maxwell in the House on Potrero Hill calls sons and
daughters off drugs and nonsense. There's justice to defend,
she says, and college to attend.

Samba of the Mission: the beat taps our feet, the heat grabs
our hips, our lips can't resist roses – in the teeth of our pos-
sibilities.

Anklet bells of South Asian women on Eddy Street, saris like bright wings at their feet.

On Divisadero, gentrification divides haves and have nots, but jazz on Fillmore survives, revives, won't die, roots are spread everywhere.

The Sutter Street YWCA is stolen property, spoils of a World War, J-Town taikos thunder: Don't forget who we are.

In the Haight, echoes of flower children, young runaways needing community — still today they cry: Spare change/change is spare.

From Geary through the Avenues, Irish Cultural Centers, Italian cafes, Russian tea shops syncopate.

The blues from Bayview: don't shut me out, baby, don't put me down . . . can barely pay my rent, baby, in this high-priced town . . . but roots are spread everywhere . . .

Harvey Milk's spirit strolls in the Castro, marches down Market. We don't forget in San Francisco.

In the Tenderloin, Cecil sings: "Love to give"
fried chicken and amazing grace,
Glide's a home, more than just a place.

On Ellis Street, double-Dutch rhymes of young men with
pride, Girls step it down and jump for joy.

sophisticated ladies, huh, check it out
well my name is Classy
and I'm more than fine
you can dial my number
baby, any time.
we got hips to move and the body grooves
we got boys to jump
when we tell them to.
we can rock the ocean
we can roll the seas
but when you mess with my man you be
boxing with me.
sophisticated ladies, huh, check it out.

—Glide Steppers

Our young people speak with complex rhythms that are real,
sublime, profound, direct. We have not dried out the music from

their language yet, as they double-Dutch, or create in poetry slams, write their lyrics on the walls, rap, or serenade us. We must allow them to define themselves, to celebrate the power of their word, to read, to write, to speak — and not concede to the heat of violence.

San Francisco is the city of poetry — a frontier for progressive poetry, a firepot for multi-ethnic poetry, an explosion of young voices creating poetry slams from this city to Washington D.C., spilling poetry into our streets. I hope to be of service this year to poetry, by working even more with our youth, by encouraging more opportunities for performances, more collaborations among poets from our diverse and multi-ethnic communities; more partnerships with the library, more festivals and technology and video events. Let us grow poetry as a means by which young people can experience the power of the word also through multi-media. And they should be the ones to lead and direct us.

I believe the poet has a responsibility to warn of dangers to our spirit. Adrienne Rich says, "We must read/write as if our lives depended upon it." And indeed our spirits are endangered if we see ourselves become numb from violence: race motivated hate crimes, anti-gay/lesbian/transgender/bi-sexual bashing, WAR. More children killing children, a glut of drugs in our poor communities, presidential candidates who make racial slurs – and we are stunned at the lack of consequence. Does Language matter? Senator McCain calls us "Gook." We as Asian Americans, and other communities of color, have experienced how language ill-used defiles, defames, dehumanizes, and incites violence. A comedian jokes: "McCain's first act if he wins the presidency will be to bomb Hanoi." Unfortunately, there's an entire swath across this country who would applaud that action.

If the power of the word penetrates deeply to our values and beliefs about who we are, and if we care about the world we wish our children to inherit, we must read, write, and vote as if our lives depended upon it. If poetry connects and humanizes and restores our souls, the power of our words must be written across the chalkboards of schools, the pages of history and literature, and the electronic pages of the future.

The University of California system hires on faculty a dismal 17% women. African-American/Hispanic/Native American student populations drastically decrease because of proposition 209, which ended affirmative action. Proposition 21 opens more jails for our youth rather than more classrooms; Proposition 22 invalidates same sex marriage. Can we sleep?

If the power of the word raises us from the slumber of complacency and warns of the powerful hatred perpetrated against people who are labeled as "different"; and if it awakens our passion for justice, we must read and write as if our lives depended upon it.

I came to poetry when I was eight years old. I wrote to save my own life, to control on the page the chaos I felt around me. In grammar school, my first poem was about the circus. I wrote about the tightrope walkers and trapeze artists.

> Circus acrobats walked
> in mid air, a miracle of balance and grace.
> flying and catching without a trace
> of fear
> with only what seemed a thread
> they hung onto life
> as they swung
> over the teeth of tigers.
> I would be frightened to fly,
> in fact, couldn't try
> with my words in a sky
> of *shhhhhhh*
> *don't tell*
> *don't cry.*

That's not quite the poem I wrote at eight. It was a long time before I could talk about my childhood abuse. Because I wanted to be acceptable, I suppressed my shame into silence, got good grades, and went to college, UCLA, and tried to fit in. In my attempts to write poetry, I was imitative of the only models we were taught – Eurocentric male poets. I did not discover Angelou, Yamamoto, Neruda, Bulosan, Robles, Tallmountain, Cervantes, Jordan, Aoki, Gomez, and Leong, or a Cecil sermon of liberation until the revolution of the '60s. I did not know I needed to give heed to that eight-year-old girl's voice until I came to work at Glide and heard the voices of children. One little girl from the Tenderloin played with matches, set her house on fire, and when they rescued her:

> She had been left alone by herself.
> On her tiny back were welts, from whippings,
> still ripe and red.
> She was in *her* darkness, setting fires,
> fighting to not extinguish her light.

At Glide, children write poetry about what home means:

> home is a gift of light bulb
> in the bathroom he must share

    in the homeless hotel, where
    monsters await to hurt him in the dark

It is here, in the poetry of young people, full of resilience and
resistance and hope, where I found that my healing occurs and
the voices of those endangered by silence are given power. We
give the gift of light in the listening, in the loving, and this, I
discovered, is the gift to ourselves. In our stories, we women
who break silences and break out of cycles of violence pay hom-
age to that eight-year-old girl's voice that could not speak.

I feel fortunate to have experienced the revolution of the '60s,
an era of political, social, cultural upheaval, and to have partici-
pated in the emergence of writers of color, our alternative press-
es that resurrected our histories and our voice. Today, especially
in San Francisco, poetry thrives as we continue our journey of
discovery and self definition – and we celebrate our
beautiful/bold/bad selves on the stage of the page:

    We, dark as plums and coffee
    light as cream and butter, gold as sun on lemons,
    red as cinnamon, brown as kola,
    plump as mangos, skinny as tallow,
    we, bad women dance without warning –

fingerpopping, hipshaking, big laughed, wisemouthed,
hefty thighed, loudtalking . . . soft syllabled,
hat wearing, tangerine lipstick queens,
fat kneed, thin ankled
WE DANCE on the same edge,
the tightrope, the high wire,
we dance with the knowledge of similar struggles:
we samba, boogie down, turgete, LEAP
from the maw of racism, sexism, homophobia, classism,
from the fire of riots and demonstrations, from ashes of
our self immolation, the addictions, abuse, the batterings

WE RISE   (Maya Angelou's refrain says)
because we would not be rooted out.
we breathe between the rain, grip deep for the winter.
we rise and realize
we have wings in our voices, because . . .

Y E S ,   W E   A R E   N O T   I N V I S I B L E

No, I'm not from Tokyo, Singapore, Saigon.
No, your dogs are safe with me.
No, I don't invade the park for squirrel meat.

No, my peripheral vision is fine.
No, I'm very bad at math.
No, I do not answer to geisha girl, china doll, mamasan,
    jap, chink or gook.
No, to us life is not cheap.
I do not know the art of tea, and no,
    I am not grateful for all you've done for me.
    Friends have died from AIDS, from PTSD
    some of us murdered, blamed for this economy
    we've been jailed for mistaken identity
    incarcerated because of ancestry
And no, I am not the model minority.
No, I am from Stockton, Angel Island, Detroit, Waikiki,
Los Angeles, San Francisco, Phoenix, New York City,
Delano, Tule Lake, Anchorage, Raleigh.
And Yes, I am alive because of memory,
    ancestors who endured adversity
    the strength of this diversity.
No, we are not invisible.
And Yes, I am from Tokyo, Singapore, Manila, Guam,
    Beijing, Cambodia, Thailand, Vietnam,
    India, Korea, Samoa, Hong Kong, Taiwan.
Yes, this strength, like ropes of the sun,
again lifts a new morning
and Yes, we rise, as always, amidst you.

I had the privilege of working with Professor June Jordan and her students at UC Berkeley in Poetry for the People Circles at Glide Church. These circles included the poor, the homeless, people in recovery programs, students, our youth, people from all walks of life. This poem was written for them while Pete Wilson was Governor of California:

POETRY FOR THE PEOPLE

Governor Wilson said he would not
increase benefits to welfare recipients
because they would "spend it on a six pack of beer."
His smile is like cold weather
as he announces: Instead, he will build more jails.

Here we huddle
in circles of poetry
against the chill of a long cold snap

we meet ourselves
in specific details of our lives

I am a woman with two children
she says, I will write down seven specific items I must buy
with my $630.00 per month AFDC check

> *rent, groceries, toilet paper, diapers, bus tokens,*
> *sanitary napkins, laundry soap*

No money left for aspirin, cookies, shoes or beer.
I put the things I want inside a heart shaped box.
> *a new dress, a bathtub full of hot water,*
> *fresh strawberries, gardenias,*
> *a warm coat, child-sized,*
> *warm hands, lover-sized.*

In circles of poetry we meet ourselves.

I am a girl with a baby, she says, writing a poem.
Do not crush this butterfly
Do not pin her wings in poverty.
Don't bruise her with teen pregnancy.
She only wants to fly
outside of hopelessness.

fly in the morning
with the breath of sea in her face
fly with the breath of God in her wings
soar above the concrete walls of a jail
and sip warm nectar from gardenias.

In circles of poetry
we meet ourselves,
tied together by the details of our lives

I am a woman with grocery list
who cannot afford strawberries,

A girl with bruises.
wings flutter
in my fist.

In this circle I meet the power of my self.

I am
a woman who opens her hand
and releases despair,
I am a poet with a pen like a river,
that springs from the mouth of my heart.
I now create my destiny.

My daughters stand on my shoulders
and see a new horizon

We are women with tongues afire,

We blaze like summer
across the sky.

See,
cold weather don't last
always.

In the U.S. a woman is physically abused every nine seconds.
Sixty-five percent of all homicides against women are related to
domestic violence, which is the primary cause of homelessness
among women and children. In the programs at Glide for young
people, we are particularly sensitive to how we might help break
the cycles of violence for children and to what messages we our-
selves may have internalized to mis-convey to them.

HIS DOMINION

He enters the room, his chest puffed.
In his hand he carries a red crayon like a weapon,
He strolls to the bookshelf, all female eyes follow.
He smiles at one,
and she, all dimples and shyness, smiles back.
He nudges another and she giggles with excitement.
He ignores another and she weeps.

Miserable, she keens for his attention.
With a single stroke,
he streaks her drawing with red crayon.
With his fisted hand,
he strikes her face, a red crayon scar on her cheek.
She stops crying now.   A smile swimming in her tears.
She is three.   He is three and a half.
She tells her mother about her day,
talking only of the boy
who destroyed her creation,
who painted her face red
with crayon, blue with bruises.
Her mother says: "That means he likes you."

THE STORM IS PASSING

for Cecil
who helps me better understand that to
love means we must strive to embrace our power
so we can have the courage to receive love.

My husband sleeps
finally,

my eyes scratchy
from lack of it.
the hospital ward
hushed, but for the steady
reassuring beep of monitors

his body has rebelled
against itself tonight
erupting in a fury
of vomit, bile
uncontainable
in the universe
of polite bedpans.

Dawn seeps
from around clouds
that have poured
all night in synchronicity
with his heaving.

In the calm of his face
I remember the
moments not of time
20 years ago

when I, wild with love,
wanted only to be at the center
of his heart
like the bee stuttering
at a peony.

Then oh, how that love
roared through seasons
wintered with rebellion
passioned in the mouth of August
between cultures of silence and shouting
between our children's resentments
the storm at our hearts raged.
I thought I searched for me, clumsy
desperate, trampling the grass.

And when the wearing of bone began,
and I saw him
with the glisten of pain in his eyes,
leaning on his bones striking bone,
naked nerves spiking his spine
I knew in fleeting flashes
he could not hide me.

Beneath the strewn leaves,
dried and dead
from autumn's breath
the root stirred, awakening.

Today, when dawn
scratches at my eyes
in this hospital bed, a thin space
between death and life,
there is my husband,
gleaming like a newborn.

In this instant
I find my presence
in morning's light
that defines the blade of grass
the tree's root,
the bee with eternal mission for its home
this heart with storm
at its center
and much room
for spring to enter.

I understood the power of the word, the power of language per-
haps most graphically when my mother broke her silence of forty
years about the World War II internment of 120,000 people of
Japanese ancestry, most of whom were American citizens – 50%
were children – in ten concentration camps throughout the
United States. She testified before the Commission on Redress
in 1981 and sent her testimony to me in the mail. It was as if in
finding her voice, she illumined the path to discover mine. I am
grateful to my mother for:

B R E A K I N G   S I L E N C E

There are miracles that happen, she said,
from the silences
in the glass caves of our ears,
from the crippled tongue,
testimonies waiting like winter.

We were told that silence was better,
useful like go quietly,
easier like don't make waves,
expedient like horse stalls, and desert camps.

Mr. Commissioner, the US Army Signal Corps

confiscated our property. It was subjected to
vandalism and ravage. I was coerced into
signing documents, giving you the authority
to take . . . to take . . .

This land, she tells, was an immigrant's hope.
Her parents cleared the ground
with only their eyes as lanterns
bare hands as plowshares

birthed fields of flowers, mustard greens
and then all was hushed for announcements:
"Take only what you can carry . . ."

We were made to believe our faces betrayed us,
our bodies were loud with yellow screaming flesh
needing to be silenced behind barbed wire.

Mr. Commissioner, it seems we were singled out from
others who were under suspicion. Our neighbors were
of German and Italian descent, some of whom were not
citizens. It seems we were singled out.

My mother wore her work like tapestry

weaving the soil with quiet roses.
And then all was hushed for announcements:
"... to be incarcerated for your own good ... "
The sounds of her work bolted in barracks, silenced.

> *Mr. Commissioner,*
> *I delivered mail in camp,*
> *carried a letter that informed an Issei couple*
> *their five sons were killed in combat serving in the US Army,*
> *serving this country that imprisons them.*
> *those memories wore like stones weighting my tongue,*

But no more ...

> So Mr. Commissioner, when you tell me my time is up,
> to sit down, to shut up,
> I tell you this:
> Pride has kept my lips pinned by nails
> my rage confined.
> But I exhume my past to claim this time.
> My youth is buried in Rohwer,
> My mother's ghost visits Amache Gate.
> My sister haunts Tule Lake.
> Words are better than tears, so I spill them,
> I kill this, the silence.

There are miracles that happen, she said,
and everything is made visible.
We speak of suicides and intimacies,
of longings lush like wet furrows,
of oceans bearing us toward imagined riches,
of burning humiliations and crimes by the governmentn
of self hate and love that breaks through silences.

We are lightening and justice
Our souls become transparent like glass
revealing tears for war-dead sons
red ashes of Hiroshima
wounds from barbed wire.

We must recognize ourselves at last.
We are a rainforest of color and noise.
We hear everything
We are unafraid.

Our language is beautiful.

Poetry connects, reconnects. Helps us to forgive ourselves, for-
give our wounds. Reunites the severed moments from mothers

and daughters and family, those details that endear us to one
another. Someone at a recent conference mentioned that her fru-
gal mother washes out ziplock plastic bags. We all laugh. My
mother washes out ziplock plastic bags, saves foil, and collects
Wendy's styrofoam cups. I laugh out loud. Now, I wash out
ziplock plastic bags, save foil. My daughter laughs out loud.

I want to tell you, my daughter,
that my love for you
extends to the children in our choir
who sing in spite of rain or bruises,
or hunger or fear of darkness.
I want to tell you, children,
of the phosphorescence of our bodies
ignited by humane touch,
by the light of our love.
It guides us, this need for each other,
like the smell of bread, the comfort of a circle,
and poetry that connects and continues
sons, daughters, your singing.

March 20, 2000

GENERATIONS OF WOMEN

I. ISSEI

Grandmother
rests, rocking to a song
she remembers from long ago.
Her same worn, blue dress
covers her knees
turned inward from weariness.
The day wears
on her shoulders that have lifted
sacks of grain and
generations of women.

She buried her husband
yesterday, incense still gathered,
in her knuckles, knotted
from the rubbings, the massage
with oils, herbs
on his swollen gouted feet,
his girded back
muscled from turning brutal rock.

She remembers
how he labored slate hard ground
to turn into her garden
draped with wisteria, lemon trees,
crimson camellias that whispered at her door.

> *Time has sucked my body.*
> *He is buried in his one black suit*
> *we kept in mothballs for this day.*
> *I want to lie next to him*
> *in my gold threaded wedding kimono,*
> *grandly purple*
> *with white cranes in flight,*
> *drape my bones with wisteria.*
> *I want to shed this century of incense*
> *resting in my pores.*
> *I want to fly with the birds on this eternal silk*
> *heading southward for their mating.*
> *I want this soil*
> *that wraps him to sleep*
> *in the smell of my work.*

Obachan
walked to the store
wearing respectable shoes –
leather hard
and painful against her sole.
She carefully fingered her coins
in the pocket of her
same blue dress
to buy sugar and yellow onions.

The clerk's single syllable spit
out a white wall   JAP.

She turned to the door
with shopping bag empty
as the sound of hard
leather, respectable
shoes that hurt her sole.

There are no tears
for moments as these.

II.   N I S E I

My mother's
body speaks,
arms long,
thin as a mantis.

> *I am afraid to leave*
> *this room of myself*
> *imprisoned by walls of cloth.*

> *My husband*
> *is indifferent, as he fingers the corners*
> *of my fabric,*
> *empty buttonholes,*
> *my muslin, grainy as a desert floor*
> *I wait for his presence.*
> *My flesh feels like bedsheets*
> *drying in the wind.*

> *This marriage by arrangement*
> *would fail, as I feared,*
> *when I saw his silk ties.*
> *His wool jackets neat*

on his full chest would not match my
wardrobe of rayon and flannel.
His smile, slick as satin,
generous to women with red lipstick.

Some losses can't be counted.
departures to desert camps
and barracks.
Men left to work in separate camps or wars.
He was gone
like his smile, slippery as satin.

She is locked in the room of her self
with worry and loneliness
barbed wire ringing her wrists,
her neck wears sorrow
like a lei of dead orchids.
She is haunted by the slaying
of a woman child.

I watched as they let her die
seventh sister born like a blue fish
into a dry orange day.
No more women, they prayed.

A son, a son, to carry on the name

Some losses can't be counted:
          years in camp, the fatal births,
          the store in Stockton, sold hastily for pittance.
          Her teeth. A marriage gone.

Abandonment left her frightened, hungry
made her count the grains of rice,
grains of desert sand,

She counts the syllables of her name.

Some prisons abide,
like the barrack inside the room
of herself,
the wind that howls
a single white syllable   JAP

There are no tears
for moments as these.

III. SANSEI

Two generations
spit me out
like uncooked rice,
one syllable words,
a woman foetus.

There are few places that are mine,
I claim them:
this ground once vandalized,
this blue silk sky where embroidered cranes keep vigil.
this opened cage of torn barbed wire,
this bowl of sand from Amache Gate.
I keep them like a rock in my shoe
to remind me
to mourn not for lost fathers,
to mend my own body
to wait not for men or marriage vows

to warn of cruel, one-syllable words,
and accusations of disloyalty.

I claim this ground where I belong,

a country with many names

I claim my place
in this line of generations of women
lean with work
soft as tea
open as the tunnels of the sea
driven as the heels of freedom's feet
taut-fisted with reparations.

Mother, Grandmother, speak in me.

I claim their strong fingers of patience,
their knees bruised with humiliation,
their hurt, longing
the sinews of their survival.

Generations of yellow women,
gather in me,
to crush the white wall
not with the wearing of sorrow,
Not with bitterness or regret.
We crush the white wall
our voices released.

We come like autumn shedding sleep
a sky about to open with rage
thunder on high rocks.
We rise like new gardens of bamboo,
our daughters are strong shoots.

There are no tears for moments as these.

I crush the white wall with my name—

    Pronounce it correctly, I say.
    Curl it on their tongue
    feel each and many syllable of it
    like grains of warm rice.

    Generations of women
    spilling each syllable
    with a loud
        yellow
                noise.

FOR A DAUGHTER WHO LEAVES

> *"More than gems in my comb box shaped by the*
> *God of the Sea, I prize you, my daughter..."*
> Lady Otomo, 8th century, Japan

A woman weaves
her daughter's wedding
slippers that will carry
her steps into a new life.
The mother weeps alone
into her jeweled sewing box
slips red thread
around its spool,
the same she used to stitch
her daughter's first silk jacket
embroidered with turtles
that would bring luck, long life.
She remembers all the steps
taken by her daughter's
unbound quick feet:
dancing on the stones
of the yard among yellow

butterflies and white breasted sparrows.
And she grew, legs strong
body long, mind
independent.
Now she captures all eyes
with her hair combed smooth
and her hips gently
swaying like bamboo.
The woman
spins her thread
from the spool of her heart,
knotted to her daughter's
departing
wedding slippers.

O S H O G A T S U

At midnight every New Years Eve,
I am boiling chicken,
onion, celery, dashi.
My husband shakes his head
in wonder at my compulsion,
my quest.
Firecrackers and whistles sound
outside our windows
as I try
to create the flavor of
Obachan's ozoni.
She had no blender, food processors,
peelers, timers, teflon.
But her ozoni,
with minced scallion,
spinach, fish,
mochi floating like a pregnant sail,
a sliver of carrot,
kiss of red radish
surprising my tongue,

was so good,
my lips pressed
on the lip of her porcelain bowl,
to savor oshogatsu.

Breath passes
and an older history
enters my mouth.

*ozoni: soup prepared with mochi or rice cake to celebrate Oshogatsu, the
New Year.

DANCING THE TWO-STEP

Honoring our mothers,
for Sandy Mori and Vicky Lee

My mother visits today,
and we talk about
harmless things,
silk stockings,
proper lengths of hems.
My daughter and I
tell her she has great legs.
For 85,
she says, they're not bad.

I remember
my mother and me
in post-war Chicago
after the camps, displaced and divorced.
She worked two jobs, made pennies with piecework.
We would go to the shoe store
and try on shoes we could not buy.
My beautiful mother with small feet
in high heel shoes and sling back straps,

would dance,
preen in the mirror,
dark eyes moist,
thinking about handsome men
who will sweep us off our feet.
And I, five years old,
in grown up shoes, stumbled
in her footsteps, needing
her forgiveness.

My mother, 85,
tells me she has great legs, for an obasan.*
Her moist eyes
are as young as the woman
in the mirror
in sling back high heels,
dancing the two step.

* an elderly woman.

S H A D O W   I N   S T O N E

Journey to Hiroshima, Japan,
International Peace Conference, 1984

We wander in the stifling heat
of August.
Hiroshima,
How you rise up
in relentless waves of heat.
      I put my mouth
on your burning sky,
on the lips of your murmuring river.
Motoyasu, River of the Dead.

      The River speaks:
      I received the bodies, leaping
      into my wet arms,
      their flesh in flame,
      and the flies that followed,
      skin rotting like wet leaves.
      My rhythm is stifled, my movement stilled.

Motoyasu cries with rituals,
bearing a thousand flickering candles
in floating lanterns of yellow, red, blue
to remember the suffering.
I light a lantern for grandmother's sister
whom they never found amidst the ashes
of your cremation.

The heat presses like many hands.
I seek solace in the stone
with human shadow burned into its face.
      I want to put my mouth to it,
to the shoulders of that body,
my tongue to wet its dusty heart.
      I ask the shadow in stone to speak:
      When I looked up
      I did not see the sun
      the kind friend who gently pulls
      the rice plants skyward.
      I worried in that moment
      if my child would find shade
      in this unbearable heat
      that melts my eyes.
      No, I did not see the sun.

I saw that day what
mankind has created
and I laid my body
into this cool stone,
my merciful resting place.

Museum of ruins.
The heat wrings our bodies
with its many fingers.
Photographs remind us of a holocaust,
and imagination stumbles, beaten, aghast.
I want to put my mouth
against these ruins: the distorted teacup,
crippled iron, melted coins,
a disfigured bowl.
I ask the bowl to speak:
The old man
held his daughter,
rocking her in his lap,
day after day after
that terrible day.
She, weak from radiation,
could not lift this bowl,
nor part her lips

as he tried to spoon okayu from this bowl,
droplet by droplet into the crack of her mouth,
the watered rice with umeboshi
which he would chew
to feed her.

He did not know
when she stopped breathing
as he put his mouth to hers,
gently to pass food.

Hiroshima, rising up.
I come here late when the weather sucks at us
I want to put my mouth
to the air, its many fingers of heat,
lick the twisted lips of a disfigured bowl,
the burned and dusty heart
of shadow in stone,
Put my mouth to the tongues of a river,
its rhythms, its living water,
weeping on the sides of lanterns,
each floating flame, a flickering
voice murmuring
over and over

as I put my mouth
to echo over and over

never again.

THE VISIT

Talking to a dying father after forty eight years of absence

I.

What did we talk about?

Your pain that is more present
because you bear it without words,
smiling with all your own straight teeth
Careful to not mention cancer that has eaten
your flesh, biting your bones.

I remember as a child, your laughter.
How I would want to put my arms around it,
My mother with too much anger
creased her mouth with criticism.
She said, after the camps, you went crazy,
chasing women in bars, and drinking up the wages,

You were desperate for laughter.

The night you left us,

you came into the bedroom,
and sang to me.
White Christmas, and the Anniversary Waltz,
weeping, sobbing, blowing your nose on my underpants.
The size of my five year old hands
could not contain the tears,
And I could not make you laugh.

When you did not return
I thought it was my fault.

2.

What did we talk about?

My daughter tells you she loves you
without guile or guilt or discomfort.
Her face is full of light, her laugh like water
as she reveals how she has become a woman
in your absence.

You close your eyes.

I could never tell you how I waited by the telephone

on Saturday nights – your "visit" night –
hair curled and redribboned, in patent leather mary janes,
and velvet dress with lace trimming.

I grew old waiting
by the silences.

3.

There was nothing to talk about.
A father lying like a plucked flower,
tumors bulbous and blue.

I did not say
I have mourned your loss for forty eight years.
Instead, desperate for laughter,
I ask if you need anything
inarisushi? a cheeseburger?

In a strand between eternities thinner
than a smile,
you laugh, straight teeth showing.

I rejoice
this conversation.

RABBIT HUNTING

After the war
we had to start over.
Get a gun
learn to listen to footsteps outside
train our dogs
keep them leashed to make them mean.

We don't want trouble
but can't bear
any more losses.

They cleaned out our barn
ravaged our house
during the war
while we were locked in barbed wire cages
laid waste the apple orchard
withered the fields that grew kale, cabbage and tomatoes.

"Not again," was all he said.

He hunts rabbits
and when he traps one, very young,

she stops and trembles.

He was born in Denver,
his parents locked up in Tule Lake Camp.
He served in the U.S. Army
as a messcook and Japanese language translator.
They called him a yellow jap
and made him taste the food before they'd eat.

Makes him so mad, these rabbits
that stop in fear
trembling.

He shoots off their heads.

K A M I K A Z E
O N   A   C L O T H E S L I N E

Chicago is the coldest place on earth
in January.

You are five years old.
A big girl. You know to knock on Mr. Utsui's door
when you come home from school.

He lives alone in a small apartment
down the hall from you and your mother,
now that his wife has died.
His only son was killed during
the war.

Mr. Utsui does not talk much,
smells like an old man,
and you don't like him
having to unlock the bathroom door
that is shared by all the third floor tenants because
neighborhood black and white kids
run up and down the stairs to use it.

You were dragged down
three flights by a big white kid who called you jap
and slant eyes.
One of the blacks rescued you
and hit that big white kid in his face.

Mama scolded you for
messing around with them who are not your kind,
and not going straight to Mr. Utsui's place.

One day, you come home from school
and it is snowing very hard
a Chicago blizzard.
Mr. Utsui isn't home and you wait
in the hallway for a long time.

You look for him
in the back yard and they
are fighting.
You are scared but can't move
frozen by the violence
between whites and blacks,
explosions of snow
spray against their bodies

as they throw fistfulls
of rock packed snowballs
through the air. The whites are winning
and chase the blacks out of the yard
and suddenly the white bully
sees you and yells to his gang,
        a jap. Let's hang the jap
        See if she can fly like a kamikaze.

You try to run but they catch you,
pull off your coat
tie your sweater sleeves around you
and hang you from the clothesline
dangling like a trussed chicken.

The boys rush to each side of the clothesline
and reel you back and forth
making airplane noises in their throats.
        kamikaze
        kamikaze
        you so crazy
        eyes so slanty
        you can't see
        so you crash and die, kamikaze.

You slide back and forth on the line
screaming and crying as the white boys laugh.

You think you will die
shivering from the cold
face numb from tears turning to ice

when you hear a loud
ooooiiii. Get away.

The boys look up and see Mr. Utsui
swinging a samurai sword around his head
as they scatter into the snow.
He unties you from the clothesline, and carries you to
his warm room, feeds you miso soup and tea
and apologizes for not being home.
He was kept waiting at the doctor's office.

Later you ask your mother
why the white boys
call you kamikaze and try to kill you,

and she tells you

Mr. Utsui lost his son
fighting in the U.S. Army, while he and his wife
were locked up in a prison camp in Arkansas.
You were in the same camp.
And when Mr. Utsui got the letter that
his son had died, he took his treasured samurai sword
and ran to the barbed wire fence
as if to cut it to pieces.
She says she thought for sure the guards
would shoot him
but they didn't.
They just laughed and called him
crazy like the kamikaze, crashing their planes
on suicide missions.

But he isn't the kamikaze, you say,
No, not the enemy, she says.

Black children
white children in a snow filled yard
shooting each other with snow balls,
American Japanese in prison camps

not the enemy.
you are not the enemy.

ROBERTA

When I was in high school one of my best friends was Roberta.

Roberta had flame red hair, a wasp waist,
voluptuous breasts and hips. Buttocks.
She had green eyes and looked like movie star Hedy Lamar.
I wanted to be Hedy Lamar
So I hung around with Roberta. She laughed at my jokes,
and I'd bring her custard filled creampuffs my mother made,
do her homework for her.

We would stand in the cafeteria line
and guys would gather around her, especially the bad boys
who wore leather jackets, chain bracelets,
and greased their hair like Elvis.
She could handle these guys with her laugh and the way she
shifted her buttocks.

I felt like a gnome. Flatchested, flatassed, invisible.
I wanted to be her. So I lathered my face with bleaching cream,
cucumbers and lemon rind.
I practiced shifting my buttocks
and kept bringing Roberta creampuffs.

One day, everyone was talking about the "nigger" who came
to school today. There weren't any blacks in our school, only ten
of us Japanese Americans.

Roberta said, what a shame they would come to our town,
why couldn't they stay where they belong? It'd be different, she
said, if they knew how to behave like us – uh, nice Orientals.

I thought I should be glad I was uh, a nice Oriental,
but I felt nauseated.

The black girl was in the hall, cornered in the stairwell,
huddled and frightened as the white girls taunted
and white boys threw paperballs, books, a jockstrap and
words more lethal than stones.

Someone in me wanted to scream at her silence
her tears and humiliation,
at the unacceptable
nobody that nobody cared about,
the nobody that nobody wanted to be.
Me. I hated her for letting me see the nobody-ness of me.

Teachers finally came and walked her out of school.

She never came back.

Roberta was standing in the cafeteria line, didn't see me,
flirting as usual with some guys, shifting her buttocks.

I thought she was laughing, talking about that black girl.
Roberta said, "She's so stupid
all teeth, dark and thick haired.
What are they doing here anyway?
But since they are clean and really studious, she comes in handy,
and her mother makes great creampuffs."

I noticed for the first time
that Roberta was a really big ass.

MOTH IN THE CLOSET

for Jody, Matthew, Phyllis

In the folds of wool sweaters,
I watch
as the young girl
hides among the shoes
in her mother's closet.

He will find her,
the large man
who smells like mash and chicken feathers.
The girl whimpers
as she hears the slapping of his slippers
entering the bedroom.

My larvae,
worm offspring
cradled in wool fiber
hears the weeping of this girl.

She presses her face into
the wall, ₋

hoping she will vanish
into the grain of wood.

Dresses
pants, shirts dance
in macabre movements on wire hangers,
as the man opens the
closet door.
empty sleeves fling
on the neck of a shirt,
unbuttoned blouses jerk and twist,
white skirt patterned with red roses
rips from its pins,
trouser fly unzips.

A child like crumpled cloth
lays on the floor
of the closet
weeping among the wrinkled flowers.

My worm
spins a cocoon
feeds from silk roses

once bloomed
on her mother's thighs.

One day,
with great dusty mothwings,
we will fly
from her closet
of empty sleeves, unfastened blouses,
and a wilted skirt of roses
watered with tears.

And every flame
shall taste
her wings.

THE STORYTELLER

for Brenda Wong Aoki
and Mark Izu

Her voice
a pool of silk
slides over our shoulders

enters our ears.

White crane maiden
weaves feathers
plucked from her heart
into a loom
of words

tsu-ka   *tsu-ka.*

A single thread, stained with blood,
is woven
into fables

of greed and love
and who prevails

Who prevails?

Sometimes we
                    fly.

BAD WOMEN

From San Francisco Women's Summit Speech
delivered on April 25, 2000

Women must change the definition we've been taught about ourselves,
and embrace our resilience that brought us through adversity. We
reject the word "bad" in its traditional meaning, referring to women
who should be silenced with shame. Instead, we are women who, in
recovery, are so good we "be BAD."

Bad women
     know how to cook
     create a miracle in a pot
     make something out of chicken feet, pigs feet, cornmeal,
     hogmaw, fishheads, fatback, ribs, roots, soy or red beans
Bad women overcome homelessness, violence, addiction and self hate.
Bad women march for equality
     education, jobs, childcare, universal health care,
     affirmative action and choice.
Bad women flaunt themselves
     plump as mangos, skinny as tallow

tall, short
dark as plums and coffee
light as cream and butter
gold as sun on lemons, red as cinnamon
brown as kola.
Bad women don't get old, they get full
full flavored like aged wine
full as harvest's vine
seasoned.
Bad women celebrate themselves,
fingerpopping, hipshaking, big laughed, wisemouthed
hefty thighed, smart thinking women
hatwearing, soft syllabled, eyelash fluttering
tangerine lipstick queens,
small and big breasted
fat kneed, skinny ankled women
who dance without warning
wrap their men or their women around their waist
and dance to the edge of dawn.
Bad women know how to stir
their tears in pots of compassion
add some hot sauce, wasabe, five spices, jalapenos
the salt of memory

stoke the fire of history
simmer in resilience
make it taste like home.

Bad women can *burn.*

DELICIOUS

In Celebration of International Women's Month,
for the women of Glide

We talk about
the beatings, your names of less-than-ness,
the invisible places you've dwelled,
without voice or shelter.

We gather where concrete walls
meet sidewalks and shattered bottles.

With the tools of our
imagination,   we chisel walls open,
plant fields of new seeds,
crops of new names.

You are cactus flower
growing in parched earth,
you are
morning glories, blooming
in the drought of profanity.

Like dandelion and lupine
you rise through cracks of concrete,
defy the crush of boot heels.

We learn to drink from the well
of our roots.

Your stems are resilient
like quince and though your limbs
ache from lifting laundry, glass ceilings and expectations,
you bend but do not break.

You are delicious,
your colors feed our hunger
the soul's creativity

Violets, elixir of sweet scented water
clover and mint made into sweet jelly
hibiscus, flaming petals sizzle into tea
and passionate lily, kissed by hummingbirds
dance in the nectar of you.

Women are the yin of romance in the yang of struggle,
the sweet and the sour in the taste buds of life

delicate and tough in the feng shui rooms of our souls.

Your voices like crops of wild strawberry
are powerful and sweet in the bowl of the world.

> *There are no downtrodden here.*
> *we gather, we women*
> *with men to reap*
> *equally in our labor*
> *and intent to love.*
> *We do this with the sun*
> *hot in our hearts,*
> *the rain cool in our breath,*
> *and the harvest abundant.*

LESSONS

I

for Amy and Clare

I thought women
carried losses
like a grocery bag
arms carefully cradling
the bottom, to prevent rupture.

I discarded the broken
eggs, bruised fruit
kept the grief
in a jar of preserves.

I discover women
who create new recipes
from ingredients
of broken eggs, and cracked precepts
about female fragility

grow herbs, stronger roots
that flavor hearty sauces

of sage, tomato
bruised papayas

serve with pasta
hot bread,
roses
an onion, whole
peeled

    layers of stamina
    layers of imagination
    layers of translucent skin

a decent cry
a damn good meal.

2

for Emma

Without Choice

we are a foot
tightly bound,
bones compressed,
deformed.

We are admired
for the beauty
of our smallness.

3

for Joyce, Lisa

This is my home   got it?

My home.
I sing in the shower
write in the kitchen

shout in the closet.

I laugh
when I want to.

Before, I didn't have
even a room.   They'd push me
against someone else's doors,
gag my mouth with their fists.

I didn't dream until Rev. Cecil said
I was worthy of dreaming.

My home.
I laugh when I want to

sing in the shower.

My sound.

G I R L F R I E N D

won't talk behind your back
       She's no backbiting
       manstealing
       you're fat talking
       bad mouthing
       telephone taping
       gossip hounding woman.

Girlfriend wants you to look good.
Drives you to the hairdressing,
       manicuring
       treadmilling
       workout place,

So you won't be
       cellulite dripping,
       raggedy hag looking
       not your best self.

Yea, she's a tell you like it is, woman.
Girlfriend listens to your secrets about

hairdying
bra stuffing
age lying
Shamefilling
molested, sex addicted secrets.
Drank too much last night
fear of failure
terror-to-succeed secrets

Girlfriend says
I did that too,
won't hold your secrets against you.
She tells you truth,
makes a cup of tea when you're blue
and if the pain gets tough,
stirs her tears into the dough
and bakes some bread for you.
Makes you laugh into your toast.

Girlfriend tells you
Women don't inhereit sorrow.
We don't have to be
painbearing
victim carrying

joy refusing
mother worrying
brow furrowing
menopause hot flashing
second sex.

Girlfriend puts you first,
has a face like mirrors,
shows the sky spreading in you,
sunlight comes through your smile
And we rejoice this love
        between friends.

A LONGER TANKA

When oak trees shed
in October air,

I remember my seeds
were thrown into a ditch,
trashed with violent words,
disregard for smaller, too sensitive
body parts.

After April,
after gentler rains,
thin tendrils of lupine,
mustard, jasmine,
a tree rooting silently,

break the still, wintered soil.

I await this warming.

YOU BRING
OUT THE "B" IN ME

On the Island of Kauai
I see surfboard, roller blade, island-wear shops
horse riding ranches, and a missionary's church
on plantations of cane

Cecil is wearing his "Love to Give from Glide" tee-shirt.
We are walking, hands entwined, looking for
anything that is run by Hawaiians
when a tanned, blond woman
in bikini, approaches him, smiling
and says: "what kind of love you gonna give me?"

I, who am apparently
invisible to her
on this plantation island, say:
>   You bring out the B word in me –
>   the big, braided muscled Hawaiian of me
>   the full blooded Asian Pacific Islander-
>   boiling ocean tsunami-
>   bursting billows of Kilauea's fire in me.

You bring out the bolt of lightning
the blazing tongue of me
    O, say can you see
    some of us are not free
    colonized still by plantation mentality.

You bring out the BE in me,
    the boundless in me:
    blissful healing of trade winds
    billowing waterfalls of hair
    belts of kukui leaves
    beloved hula of our arms
    blessings of my grandmother's journey
    the blood of her hands in this black coffee soil,
    brave generations breaking chains of greed.

You bring out the B word in me
A burnishing sunrise BE-ing in me
A bridge of visible Beauty
that spans even chasms of bigotry.

And all will see
the be in me

be beautiful
brilliant
bold,
be bad brown/yellow woman
beside her man
with real love to give.

S O U L   F O O D

f o r   C e c i l

We prepare
the meal together.
I complain,
hurt, reduced to fury
again by their
subtle insults,
insinuations
because I am married to you,
impossible autonomy, no mind
of my own.

You like your fish
crisp, coated with cornmeal,
fried deep,
sliced mangos to sweeten
the tang of lemons.
My fish is raw.
on shredded lettuce,

lemon slices thin as skin,
wasabe burning like green fire.
You bake the cornbread flat
and dip it in
the thick soup
I've brewed from
turkey carcass, rice gruel,
sesame oil and chervil.
We laugh over watermelon
and bubbling cobbler.

You say
There are few men
who can stand
to have a woman equal,
upright.

This meal,
unsurpassed.

IRON BUTTERFLY

Silk, iron
iron, silk
flesh, feather
window, open
silk wing
iron butterfly.

I am all of these, silk wings
iron butterfly.
I recover myself from the wasteland of invisible,
from dark closets, banished there when I was a child
for crimes I did not understand.
Shame locked me in prisons of silence.
Language was incest's enemy
                    shhhh...

I grew up hungry
seeking men with hands of metal
a familiar violence
and pain that fit well.
In this journey of bruised woman without speech,

I came upon a church where God loves
criminals and samaritans alike.
A minister shouts to me,
I accept you, unconditionally

Love, he says, awakens us from the dead,
And I in circles of recovery
discovered my tongue in the mouths
of women telling stories
changing whispers of shame and sorry
to shouts for justice, truth, release.
      Here is hope, in community,
where diversity is alive,
men/women in mutuality,
breaking cycles of injury
and children speak in poetry.
      Here is hope *love transforms.*
She who was banished to closet and beating floor,
background, backseat
no longer whimpers, but sings.

      This is she/me—who dared not
to laugh out loud.

I see light burst into her mouth.

I am open window
I am bird of paradise
I am iron butterfly
I am flesh and blood and silk wings
rising up from dead bones,
dancing in the music of our words.

      Butterflies cannot resist her symphony of color
      they drink from her amber
      the nectar she makes from the plum of herself.

I am she/we
of flesh
and iron
and silk wings,
healing,   flying
into a gentle   blue sky.

THE SINGING

Inspired by *Phoenix Eyes* by Russell Leong
In commemoration of World AIDS Day, 2000

You begin in Water
    distilled in the cup of a lotus,
    drink,   dream of love
    longing for flesh
    eat petals and fall to the
Earth
    dissolve to sea
    rise to
Air
    once more
Rain

    ritual
    chant
    the singing

You tell of sons
in rooms that are silent and sick

and families who do not claim them,
leave white deli cartons of food outside closed doors.
  tuberculosis, cancer, leukemia, name it anything else.

This disease of AIDS
calls us.

You tell of violence:
the longing of men
the prison of what was thought as love,
the quest for release.

You invite us close to the fire
to let us hear the singing.

Nothing of life is a waste
  *Rain does not return to heaven until it waters earth. **

You tell of violation:
women with eyebrows like butterfly wings
are sold into sex slavery,
they are like acrobats,

*Isaiah 55:10

bodies suspended in silk
adapt to mutilation.
Disease flutters on their lips.

For survival, they place their passion
in perfume bottles and opium pipes,

and still there is the singing.

With the discipline of a monk
you walk
through colonies of America
to the villages of China
carve this journey into our skin:

> *Watts, Kearny Street/San Francisco,*
> *Jasper, Phoenix, Tule Lake, Selma,*
> *Diem Bien Phu, Manila, Hiroshima,*
> *Tiananmen, SubSahara/Africa, Saigon*

The tip of your pen, sharper than a knife
cut bindings from the perfectly small foot,
remove fishhook from a hungry mouth,
slice ginger for a feast.

Doors open.
Rain is music descending,
rising.

We hear the singing
and the dialect
of your poems that steam from pages
like water alight with fire.

You claim our sons. They have not disappeared.

Daughters with butterfly brows,
hold the strength of the flame,
an eternal resurrection.

Looking for America
looking for a home
that smells of fish and rice
and sounds of a banjo.

They found the I Hotel
lined with sweat and bone
and here they sang and slept,
on Kearny Street their home.

GHOST OF THE I HOTEL

for Al Robles and the
Manongs of Manilatown

Ghost of manongs
ghost of cannery workers
farmworkers, sweatshop workers, poets.
Ghost of I Hotel
was buried in an excavated hole.
Her old skin
smells of coconut and fish,
her bruised flesh
punctured and sledgehammered,
battered with billy clubs and bootheels.

We come back to this gravesite,
this hole on Kearny Street
where once we marched
and watched her fall
beneath indifferent profiteers,
Ghosts rise,
reminding us there are few places
that are ours.
Beneath this broken ground
are buried dreams of an America
with open doors, justice.
Manong Laurencio sits in the lobby at Glide Church
on fried chicken day
smiles, waves
calls the Reverend Cecil, "Father."
Tells me he is never full
but here he comes to eat so much
his hunger like his eyes,
wide bowls filled but never full.
The food is good. The Father is good.
Friends come here too.   But hungry still.
Perhaps it is because in the Tenderloin
the streets do not flow with soy sauce.
He does not smell fishheads,

no lumpia, rice
adobo, jars of bagoong
to bring home to his cold room.
Mango trees do not grow on wine stained concrete.
No pool halls,
barbershops where legends and laughter
sing like gold banjos.
Instead, his eyes are moist
and dark with fear of becoming sick,
of losing food stamps and shelter.
He says sad manongs are scattered like
old leaves in the wind.

> *Gather me in the smell of*
> *old wood*
> *in the arms*
> *of taxi dancers.*
> *In the tall grass*
> *near my village*
> *gather me in memory*
> *and let me chew rice with new teeth*
> *lick my fingers*
> *as the juices of roast pig*
> *soak my lips.*

Gather me in the rooms
of International Hotel,
born again in the fog,
in the shadow of a bridge.

International Hotel lies in the heart
of Delano farmfields and Agbayani village
Alaskan Canneries and Ifugao Mountains.
International Hotel rises,
in poetry of Manong Al Robles,
    Norman Jayo, Luis Syquia, Serafin.
Resilient as bamboo,
irresistible as revolution –
    Manong Laurencio, Jose,
    Wahat, Federico, Legaspi, Diones,
    your stories, legends, laughter
    live again.
        Come, and eat
        come, and eat
        fill up the bowls of your eyes
        with mango trees
        and you will not be hungry.

APPETITE

You are
an animal

will not sit still
not behave

Release yourself
indiscreetly
burst into good company
sniff in the wrong places
and embarrass people.

Your appetite
curls around each morsel –

> the sour, curdled
> syllables of ra cism
> the pungent consonants
> of terr ibletruth.

Savors
    sweet sorbet
    melting on you, tongue

    when your beloved
    strokes you
    with the gentle vowel
    sounds of
    l uu v.

WHAT IS POSSIBLE

for Jeannine

One year older, I remember less
but images that remain
give much pleasure

conversations of your hands, speaking
to a deaf aunt
describe a ginkgo tree
planted by your father
in the backyard.

The dance of your hands
soft light from your face
your long limbs leaning into white spaces
help me imagine
what is possible
to be grown from love.

> Some women
> live with their arms crossed
> to hide shame

hold fear tightly.
Without full measure of light
fruit turns small and bitter.

Some women
like orchards, grow
heartily despite winter,
planted deep
strongly rooted
her seed tendrils stretch, branches spread.
In elegant ripeness
are released leaf, fan, fragrance, fruit.

It is possible
to find comfort in hands
opening   gentle
as shade.

SOLDIER

for June Jordan
on reading her
autobiography, *Soldier*

Whack!
She hits back
the tennis ball.

And whack!
Smashes into his body
before he can blink.

It is a small ball
Light, hollow
But it hurts
unexpected
like a fist

> Words compacted
> like a fist.
> June's poetry.

Speed
Velocity
Angle of impact
Perception
Timing

    warn those who
    would attempt to dominate
    diminish
    destroy a woman

    She who survives
    has honed awareness
    keen instinct, night vision
    strength

    a hunger
    for justice.

He does not know
who he has trained.

Whack!

a woman poet.

NOT SILENT

for Ntombi

It is clear
you did not come to San Francisco
to be silent or passive
like some ripe bruise
on a woman's neck.

You don't smother
your spirit
like some sideways glance
of a frightened child
waiting to be slapped.

You don't cover up your
light like someone battered
into bleak invisiblity.

You don't roll yourself up
like a sidewalk sleeping
homeless person cocooned on cold concrete.

On this graduation day
proud with letters of M.A.

You open your memory
 and tell me you wish your father
could see you in this moment
of excellence
    because he could
    stand on a cloud
    larger than life
    radiating with strength
    hold you in the arms of his courage
    those same strong arms
    that slapped you unconscious.

It is never a simple matter
this raging love, this unwanted hunger.

    I tell you of the man
    who in heroic moments
    refused to shake a racist's hand
    who kicked me against the wall
    for laughing too loud.

How confused our lusts become
in the corners of childhood.

But you did not come here
to remain silent, you
honored your beauty
honored the voice that shattered
the bottles containing oblivion,
graduated to the circle
of singers.

> *You witness*
> *to those bruises that are*
> *the same on the women*
> *who surround you.*
> *They stretch throats*
> *to heaven, repairing, releasing*
> *strangleholds of shame.*

> *Children and homeless*
> *sleepers*
> *dulled by pain*
> *awaken to hope.*
> *Sidewalks dance.*

You graduate.   The circle
of healers, weavers, singers
players of violins
poets, dragqueens, female children
unfold themselves
like waves of music,
sunlight stretched on the streets.

You did not come here
to be silent.

JANICE MIRIKITANI has lived in San Francisco since 1963. As Executive Director and President of Glide Foundation, she has created and directed programs at Glide Memorial Church for over thirty-five years. She is the author of three books of poetry and has edited several anthologies of poetry and prose.

THE POET LAUREATE SERIES is made possible by support from San Francisco Grants for the Arts, the ArtCouncil, the Zellerbach Fund, and the W.A. Gerbode Fund.

CITY LIGHTS FOUNDATION is a nonprofit foundation that supports literacy and the literary arts.

All contributions are gratefully accepted and fully tax deductible.

P.O. Box 33207, San Francisco California 94133
www.citylights.com
staff@citylights.com